Works of Wildfire

Works of Wildfire
poems
Eleanor Berry

GRAYSON BOOKS
West Hartford, Connecticut
graysonbooks.com

Works of Wildfire
copyright © 2022 by Eleanor Berry
published by Grayson Books
West Hartford, Connecticut
ISBN: 978-0-9675554-7-8

Book and Cover Design: Cindy Stewart
Cover Art: Margaret Godfrey, Burnt Bark and Burned Trio (fragment)
Author Photo: Thanks to Richard Berry

Acknowledgments

Grateful acknowledgment is made to the editors of the following publications, in which the listed poems first appeared.

The Madrona Project II.2 (2022), issue on the theme of "Human Communities in Wild Places": "Stance"

Windfall: A Journal of Poetry of Place 20.1 (2021): "Landscape of Fire"

The latter two sections of "Landscape of Fire" (under the title "When you enter the fire zone, forget") and the full texts of "Leaves," "Out of Burned Land," and "The place we left" were incorporated in *LAND SCAPE SHIFT*, an installation with artist Ann Kresge, which was part of an exhibit of collaborative works by poets and visual artists at the Bush Barn Art Center, Salem, Oregon, January 14-February 26, 2022. The installation included a recorded reading of these poems, wall-mounted excerpts, and 25 copies of a handstitched booklet, *A Fascicle from Fire*, with original-print covers and endpapers.

Think
what got away in my life
was enough to see me through
    – Lorine Niedecker

"It is your relationship to the beautiful, not the beautiful thing by itself, that carries you," said Grizzly Bear.
    – Barry Lopez

For Richard, who knows we live more in our minds
than in physical places, yet whose photographs
hold much of our lives

And for the friends who knew and gave
what we needed to begin again—again

Contents

When we left without you, we opened the barn gates into your pasture	11
Synecdoche	13
Stance	14
Landscape of Fire	16
Forest	18
Strange Ecstasy	20
Works of Fire	21
I Thought They Would Outlast Me	23
Leaves	24
A Monologue Addressed to W. B. Yeats	28
Fireweed	30
Out of Burned Land	31
The place we left	33
Coda: What luck,	35
In Gratitude	37
About the Author	41

When we left without you, we opened the barn gates into your pasture

for alpacas Vega, Jackson, and Silverado

The field is ringed by fire,
by fir trees turned torches.
The barn is ablaze.

In the fire-ringed field
the drought-dried grass
singes and chars, but
you've grazed it so short
it doesn't flame up.

In the middle of the field
is a hollowed-out place of
bare dirt and stones—
at the center of the field
a scooped-out bowl with
nothing to burn.

You know that place well.
Find your way to it
through the dark and thick smoke,
through the wind-driven
rain of sparks.

Hunker there, where you
have rolled to loosen burs,
slough off flies, or just
to feel the earth
through your fleece.

You have nothing
any more to fear
from coyotes denned beneath the hill,
their nightly chorus silenced
as the fire swept up-slope.

You know to seek
that hollowed-out place
at the center of the field
ringed by fire, which
will rage all around you but
cannot reach you there.

Be, in the midst of fire-kill,
living creatures still.

Synecdoche
> *a figure of speech in which a part of something is used to refer to the whole*

House, house, house...
narrates the driver
in a video shot as his car
follows the road up
where wildfire swept down.
He means: Here and here and here
a house was.

Chimney, chimney, chimney...
is all the camera sees.
Hi-ho, the derry-o
The cheese stands alone
but on lot after lot after lot,
it's the chimney
stands alone.

Fitting, I suppose, because
hearth is a common
synecdoche for *home*,
and every hearth
requires a chimney.
When mantel and ceiling and walls
have collapsed, flaming, into
the foundation,
and burnt down to a thick
stratum of ash,
when heat far greater
than concrete can resist
has left it spalled and cracked,
only the chimney
stands as before.

Stance

Squirrel-size, this black cast-iron pig,
which sat by the woodstove like a small
protective household god—now that wildfire
vastly larger and fiercer than any blaze
ever kindled in that stove
has left of the house only its stone chimney—
still sits on its haunches as if patiently waiting.

The gloss of its black paint has dulled, the tip
of one ear looks chewed off, and one eye
appears as if blinded. The seam between
the halves of the casting has gaped apart.
The stance that bespoke aliveness
now tells what comes of being trapped
in a maelstrom of fire, even
if one is made of metal.

But if one is made only of mettle,
of mettle imbued
in flesh, in muscle and tendon, if one is
not a squirrel-size figure but a squirrel
and trapped in a maelstrom of fire, oh then
one is changed
to an effigy of squirrel
as fixed in its stance—upright on hindlegs,
braced to scan for any route of escape—
as the cast-iron pig
and, except for one pinkish-gray protruding loop
of intestine, perfectly
carbon-black.

~

Lift the carbonized squirrel
gently from the ground. Wrap
the small, stiff body
in paper towels. Then spade
as best you can amid the roots
of the scorched firs
a squirrel-sized grave, and set therein
the charred corpse wound with its makeshift shroud.
Mound the scooped-out dirt
back over it, and lightly
tamp it down.

Lift the cast-iron pig
gently from the rubble of the hearth.
With a whisk broom, brush off
the clinging film of ash. Then buff
the metal with a wire brush.
Take the pig with you to your temporary home
to be, no longer a guardian, but, like a working dog
grown too stiff-jointed and dim-sighted
for his duties, simply a companion.

Landscape of Fire

Fall is a slow painter, taking weeks to overlay
the maples' green with gold, to turn the dwarf euonymus
scarlet leaf by leaf, to daub each sweet gum's crown
an intricate mottle of crimson, ochre, dun, and bronze.
Fall never finishes a piece, every morning
paints over the work of the day before—
deepening hues here, lightening others there.

Fire works fast—turns out a whole landscape
overnight. But do not say there is
no beauty in its palette of
ash, soot, rust, char.

~

Tropical eyes must adjust to see
abundance in a temperate zone;
forest hearts must stretch to feel
peace on the prairie; and island people,
when they come to the continent,
must learn to sense that it, too,
is land amid the sea.

So to find beauty in a landscape of fire,
you must look with a new mind.

~

When you enter the fire zone, forget
what you thought you knew of the place
where you had your home. Forget

its canopy of deep teal green—
the high boughs of Douglas-fir—
interspersed with citron and
sienna brown—the autumn hues
of big-leaf maple, Garry oak. Forget

its understory thickets, their
little leaves, each kind
uniquely shaped and edged.

All those leaves are gone, all
the evergreen needles
turned to rust.

~

When you enter the fire zone, summon
to mind the paintings ancient humans left
on cave walls. Fire must have taken
its palette from them. Even the sky
has that red-ochre hue.

Let the new landscape teach you
an aesthetic of monochrome,
its difficult austerities.

Forest

Their trunks were tall and straight
limber and long their many boughs.
Wind woke them into wild dance.

Come spring, each slightest breeze
shook loose their pollen cones, piling
a damp quilt on the sprouting grass.
Each fall their seed cones, ripened,
bombarded the ground.
All year their crowns remained
deep teal green.

In height and girth they'd grown
tier on tier of branches,
ring after ring of wood,
some thirty years or more.

~

For one late-summer night
they blazed, mammoth torches
amid the dark—to be left

black columns, sparse crowns
blizzarding singed needles, covering
ash-mulched earth
with rust-colored snow.

Beneath their carbonized bark,
the fire-killed trees
still keep sound wood, fit
for salvage logging—

forced harvest before
bark beetles infest.

~

Felled and staged for loading
onto the logger's truck, they're
decapitated trunks, stripped
of side branches. They lie
in massive stacks about the land,
now nearly treeless, which
they had made forest.

Strange Ecstasy

    for Paul Toews

Thank you, old friend—friend
in loving untamed land, in making art,
friend also now
in losing to wildfire
house and all the woods around it—
thank you for saying
what I've thought but not dared speak:

Those who would console us
seem to feel our loss
more than we do. They weep
while our eyes
stay dry.

Not quite your words, but what
I heard you say.... When a friend from town
dissolved in tears the instant she saw
the rubble that had been
our house, I felt—absurdly, I realized—
robbed of the loss
I hadn't yet begun to mourn.

The loss is ours, and we feel it, yet somehow
stand outside our own feeling. That's
ecstasy—or at least what the Greek
it comes from, *ekstasis*, means—
outside stance. A strange
ecstasy indeed, but how else
could we go on
with the work?

Works of Fire

Heated far above its melting point,
the lawn tractor's aluminum engine
has flowed down and pooled
beneath the carcass of the chassis.
Cooled and re-hardened, it's a glyph
in a system of writing
no one yet knows.

The one-liter graduated cylinder,
bargain buy years back
from a lab equipment surplus store,
no longer measures, or even holds,
volumes of liquid. No longer
a vessel, it's become
a vitreous scrunch-boot
no one can wear.

The magnet assembly of the seismometer,
set up to detect tremors that might
herald "the big one," has been
left to stand on its own—
short lad with stout legs.

Refired in an inferno of blazing walls,
the celadon-glazed sauceboat
an artist ancestor once used
for rinsing her brushes
has emerged rough-surfaced
a deep, iridescent magenta

Freed of their words, the books'
layers on layers of pages
are so much ghost mica.

At a touch they turn
to white clay powder.

~

Now you must dig,
archaeologist in the ashpit
Fire has made of your home.

Now you must become
curator of all the objects—
familiar, dear, or half-forgotten—
Fire has given new forms.

I Thought They Would Outlast Me

Recalling the welter of thrift-store finds crowding a friend's small apartment when we were both young, I remember how I imagined then that each thing bore its history of touch—each had been held, used, set down, discreetly hidden away by others' hands. I imagined layerings of touch, building an invisible patina.

What strikes me now is how each object's place in an intricate story is lost when it passes from one person's hands to another's—another who has no inkling what fancies and memories had wrapped it round. I envision strippings, meanings torn off like burning garments, leaving a raw and sudden nakedness.

~

So I wrote, secure a quarter-century in one home, surrounded there by objects my eyes caressed, my mind held dear. I feared for them—cast adrift at my death, or sooner, if my faculties failed. When I can no longer hold them, even in mind, I fretted, what will become of them?

Now, that home gone overnight to wildfire, the things I looked at fondly every day are nowhere—unless they're held in mind—in my mind, in the minds of their makers, their past owners, in the minds of friends who noticed them on visits, the minds of those who came to do household repairs, and glanced around the rooms through which they passed.

Leaves

How to read these leaves

      not tea leaves or
      tree leaves (those all
      burnt in an instant to ash)

      not whole leaves
      of books either (only
      white clay powder
      left from the thousands
      once on our shelves—
      except for these...)

these half-dozen pale
char-edged ovals of
heat-crisped paper
scattered amid
skeletons of bushes and
blackened trunks of firs

      not portrait ovals (like
      the fading photograph of
      her father that my mother kept
      in an oval tin frame
      on a bureau across
      from her bed)

but broad ovals—
centers of pages
from a landscape-format book—

      not the *Divine Comedy* or
      the complete plays

　　　　of Shakespeare, not
　　　　the *Atlas of the Heavens*

　　　　but (Fire
　　　　being an ironist)
　　　　The Reader's Digest
　　　　Guide to Gardening

—flimsy discs of paper that
escaped the flames,
blew free and scattered,
when that book burned
from the outside in

How to read these leaves

　　　　　singed paper printed
　　　　　recto and verso (though
　　　　　no way now to tell
　　　　　which was which
　　　　　and only guesswork
　　　　　to infer their order)

these fragments—
text and line-drawings—
that alone remain
from our house of books

How to take, amid the sudden
wreckage

　　　　　their advice on repairing
　　　　　a lawn, on selecting shrubs,
　　　　　on pruning

    their list of insect pests
    with signs of each and
    chemicals to combat it

    their descriptions of species that
    grow well in wet places, their
    account of the uses and
    types of house plants, their
    guide to propagating cacti

here in this black and cinder-gray
wildfire landscape, under a sky
glowering rust-red

    here where we lived amid
    shrub and flower borders eked
    from rocky soil, native plants
    tenderly nursed, vigorous invasives
    yearly cut down and pulled out
    only to surge back, decades-old
    stands of firs, multi-trunked
    maples and oaks, pasture
    fenced and cross-fenced, new bridge
    over the seasonal creek

how to take these random remnants
of gardening guidance except
as a sardonic reminder:
All is vanity

    unless, perhaps,
    as haphazard hints
    to a way beyond:

> *Begin again by watching*
> *what returns (tending frail shoots,*
> *wresting out robust weeds)*
> *Begin again by planting*

And what to make of this:

> On one flame-spared
> page-scrap, no words, only a
> delicate line-drawing
> of an orchid, perfectly fitting within
> the oval that Fire had cut

A Monologue Addressed to W. B. Yeats

Your lines, William Yeats, rise to mind
some sixty years after I first
read them in the *Collected Poems*
my future father brought home
from the war in the Pacific, volume
lent him by a pilot friend whose plane
didn't return. For me, the dark
clothbound book on my father's shelves held
a tragic glamor, and the lines that surge up now
reflect your own attunement to such
pregnant doom and its pervasive
presence in your English-ruled
Ireland of a century ago:

A terrible beauty is born.
I'd never even heard the term
oxymoron, let alone
learned its meaning.
I knew nothing of the Easter Rebellion,
had never felt the shock of
half-despised, casual friends
suddenly become martyrs
for a cause I shared. But that refrain
of your "Easter 1916" stirred me with a sense
of a truth beyond the compass
of my small experience.

A terrible beauty is born.
Now when I confront
what wildfire has made
of house and yard, woodlot and barn,
that line of yours
is all I know to say.

All things fall and are built again...
I'd never heard the term
ekphrasis, had no inkling
of the long tradition of poetry
about visual art.
"Lapis Lazuli" I heard
only as lovely sounds, didn't realize
the title of that meditative poem
named the stone of the carving
that occasioned it. The three
aged Chinese sages at the end
I didn't see as sculpture. They were
vivid figures in a world more real
than the one in which I sat and read.
Curious that their clifftop view
resonated so deeply with me, who then
had neither years nor mountains
from which to gaze.

*All things fall and are built again
and those that build them again
are gay....* I hadn't yet known
disaster or its aftermath. But those lines,
with gay in its old sense of *joyous*,
have stayed with me, to serve now
as something between admonition
and inspiration: ...*gaiety transfiguring
all that dread.*

Fireweed

If there had been no fire, these seeds,
years in the soil,
would not have sprouted.

If fire had not opened
the land to sunlight, these shoots
would not have emerged, lengthened,
leafed out, and bloomed.

But for the fire, these tall
clusters of four-petalled
magenta flowers, each offering up
its four pollen-laden anthers and
its nectar-beaded, four-cleft stigma,
would not festoon this land.

As the days shorten and the sunlight
begins to fall aslant, the fine
white silk of thousands
of new seeds would not dazzle,

backlit, against the piles
of charred slash.

Out of Burned Land

Perennials

Against the gray-black
tangle of scorched shrubs, white
Canterbury bells, profuse
as they never were
beneath the shade of firs—
they shrivel in a single day
of unremitting sun.

Reforestation

Mullein stalks rise as straight
as Doug fir trunks, though
shorter by far, and
set to topple after
a single season.

Harbinger?

Its pretty yellow blossoms
catch my eye, but
this scrubby, ankle-high plant
is completely sheathed
in spines. Buffalo bur's native
to arid waste.

Annuals

Where different flowers every year
ringed the birdbath, petunias open
bright magenta out of
cinder-gray, and from years back

a sole lobelia
startles with sapphire.

Volunteer Sapling

Amid the thick brush
of weeds gone to seed, this slender
woody stalk, erect with a few
wide-spaced thorns, delicate
pinnate leaves. A half mile
down the road, last spring as ever
a grove of locust trees
diffused the fragrance of its blooms.

Harvest

From vines sprouted
where the compost was,
four perfect delicata squash

The place we left

is no longer the place we left.

Soon after we fled that night, the shaggy spires of firs
must have become so many fifty-foot torches.

When we first went back, we found
charred-black trunks raining down
dead needles.

Salvage logging turned the burned woods into
stump-fields, into gouged earth strewn
with hacked-off fir-limbs
and studded with a few
clumsy heaps of slash.

Now, nearly a year since the fire, the ravaged land
hosts a battalion of mullein—dozens of coarse,
eye-level stalks—where past years
firs canopied native shrubs.

~

The place we left
is no longer the place we left, no longer

our address. We chose not
to rebuild in that changed place, instead moved
to this 1950s subdivision between
old orchards and town.

How calmly the single-story houses
stretch out on their shrub-bordered lots!

On the wires overhead, plump doves
proclaim territory.

Does anyone here know
how swiftly and completely
a long-familiar landscape
can be undone?

Coda

What luck,

we said. The acres we'd bought
some two decades back and made our home
happened to lie right in the path
of a total solar eclipse, barely a quarter mile
from the centerline. No need to travel
across the world to view it, no need even
to leave our land—if only
persistent smoke from distant wildfires
dispersed on the awaited day. What luck
that it did, just in time for us to witness
the entire eclipse, from first
contact to last.

                Three years after we watched,
in the sky above our familiar home horizon,
a pale radiance appear around the sun's
briefly moon-blocked disk, this same land of ours
would lie right in the path
of record winds from the east, bellows
to smoldering fires in steep, remote terrain,
fanning them high, driving a storm of embers
swiftly west and down the canyon, setting
drought-parched trees and brush alight, igniting
anything wood-built. The swath of burn
reached barely a quarter mile
past our place, when the wind, forecast
to continue hours longer, abruptly stopped.
What luck for those whose homes were spared.

Fir trees blackened and dead,
house, out-buildings, and all
their contents consumed, this land
is no longer our homesite, but remains
ours in the tax rolls. Land that was—
until it was seized by settlers, whence it came,
through a long succession of sales, to us—
part of the home of the Santiam Band
of Kalapuya. Each year for centuries,
they burned off underbrush, kept open
camas meadows for harvest, never left
these acres stoked with fuel for wildfire,
kept open a view of the sky.

                        What luck
if, in the strip of low, wet meadow running
the length of this land—meadow long thick with
weed blackberry and dock, now suddenly cleared
by wildfire and earthmover—
camas comes to bloom again.

In Gratitude

I am fortunate to have been a member of The Peregrine Writers, a poetry critique group based in Salem, Oregon, since its founding more than 20 years ago. I am grateful to all its present members—Lois Rosen, Ada Molinoff, Colette Tennant, Stephanie Lenox, Dina Triest, Penina Taesali, Steve Slemenda, and Paul Suter—for their attentive readings of early drafts of these poems and for their encouragement of my efforts to order them into a larger whole.

To write and compile the poems in this chapbook, however, I needed more than the thoughtful critiques of fellow poets. In the wake of the wildfire that destroyed our home, among hundreds of others in Western Oregon's Santiam Canyon, my husband and I needed first to be given basic elements of everyday life—a place to stay, clothes, food ready to eat or with means to prepare it. This chapbook was made possible by the poet friends who provided us all that and more: by Dina Triest, who invited us to stay in an apartment in her house, where we ultimately remained for seven months; by Susan and Joe Morse, who brought us bags of groceries, a teakettle, a fan, and a computer mouse; by Ada Molinoff, who assembled the start of a new wardrobe for me; by Dina and by Colette Tennant, who brought us delicious baked treats and small *objets d'art*; by Lois Rosen, who sent us delightful care packages of pretty and practical things; and by all the friends, too many to name here, who sent cards and messages of support.

The fire had taken far more than furniture, appliances, and household "stuff." It had taken books and art gathered over fifty years. The books included an extensive personal library of poetry, especially strong in Oregon poetry and 20th-century American poetry. To write, I needed the companionship of those volumes of predecessors' and contemporaries' work. For filling that need, I am grateful to many poet friends: to Don Colburn, who bought several copies of my chapbook *Only So Far* and sent them to me along with a thoughtful selection of other poets' books that had been on my burned bookshelves; to Paul Merchant brought me cartons of books by Oregon and other American poets from his own personal library; to Penina Taesali, who collected donations of poetry books from fellow Oregon poets and supplemented them with many literary treasures from her own shelves; to those poets, too many to name here, who gave me books through Penina; to Ingrid Wendt, who replaced all of her books and those of her late husband, Ralph Salisbury, which I had bought as they were published, and greatly valued; to Mark Janssen and Marilyn Johnston, who brought culls from their shelves as well copies of their own new or recent books; to Charmaine Pappas Donovan, Joseph Cavanaugh, and Julie Cummings, friends from other state poetry societies, who sent me packages of poetry books from across the country; to the late Erik Muller, publisher of my first book of poetry, who sent me what would be his last collection of his own poems and his last volume of appreciative analysis of another poet's work, and who, while in home hospice, set aside books from his personal library to help replenish mine; to Nancy Christopherson, who sent me the two-volume *Collected Poems* of William Carlos Williams, all of whose poetry I'd had in various editions and from which I'd learned much of what I know of free-verse prosody.

Like Williams, I've long had a strong affinity for visual art, and much of my poetry, whether ekphrastic or not, has been inspired by art on the walls around me. The walls of our house that burned had been covered artworks, many by friends; the walls of our new house were strangely empty. I am grateful to the friends who helped me to begin making our new rooms places where art keeps me company: to Cynthia Herron, who, even before we moved into our new house, invited us to choose paintings from her home studio; to Dina Triest and Colette Tennant, both of whom gave me paintings by our mutual friend, the late Virginia Corrie-Cozart, to help fill the loss of ones I'd treasured; to Toni Kramer and Steve Kenyon, who replaced a print I'd loved of a Diebenkorn "Seated Woman" painting with one from their own walls; to Becki Hesedahl, who painted a new version of a watercolor of hers that had hung in my old study, and delivered it to us, framed and ready to hang in my new study; to Paul Merchant and Steve Tilden, who replaced one of Steve's metal "translations" of Paul's poetry that had hung in our old living room with one that now hangs in our new one; to Willa Schneberg, who gave us one of her "Flood Book" series of ceramic sculptures to replace one that had, ironically, been lost in the fire that destroyed our old house; to Susan Appleby, one of whose paintings was the cover art for my previous chapbook and who refused payment for a print of another of her paintings, which I am looking up at as I type these words.

I am grateful also to Paul Toews, whose own home and studio, with many new paintings, was also destroyed in the Beachie Creek Fire, for devising with me a program of poetry, art, storytelling, and music on the theme of "Wildfire in a Time of Climate Change," where several of these poems were first performed; and to Ann Kresge, for partnering with me in a year-long collaboration that culminated in *Land Scape Shift*, an installation exploring, through interrelated poems and visual works, our responses to stark changes in our home landscapes.

Food, shelter, and clothing; books and art: I couldn't have written these poems without all that friends did to ensure that I had both these different sorts of necessities. And not only these but plants and birds around me and useful things that it's a pleasure to use. I'm grateful to Penina Taesali for bringing me not only books but plants and bird feeders, wall decorations, and the first "poet dresses" I'd had since the fire; to Lynn Takata for giving me not only a fleece pullover, but a native shrub that's now flourishing in our new backyard; to Robin Christy Humelbaugh and Jacqui Jenkins for beautiful sets of dishes; to John Larimer for many inspired gifts, but especially for seedlings and seeds that enabled us to plant a vegetable garden.

My husband, Richard Berry, has been both a partner in all the challenges that "total loss" poses and a companion in responding to the experience through creative work. The photography he has done of the fire's devastation and of its long aftermath has inspired and informed my poetry, and his love and support have sustained me in both the living and the writing.

About the Author

Eleanor Berry and her husband lived on rural land in the Santiam Canyon east of Salem, Oregon, from 1994 until Labor Day 2020, when their house, outbuildings, and woods were destroyed in the Beachie Creek fire. Berry has two books of poetry, *Green November* (2007) and *No Constant Hues* (2015), both from Oregon independent publishers, and a chapbook, *Only So Far* (2019), from Main Street Rag. A past president of the Oregon Poetry Association and the National Federation of State Poetry Societies, Berry has taught literature and writing at several colleges and universities. Her essays on 20th-century American poetry and free verse prosody have been published in various scholarly journals, and her poems have appeared in numerous literary magazines and several anthologies.

www.ingramcontent.com/pod-product-compliance
Lightning Source LLC
Chambersburg PA
CBHW032053290426
44110CB00012B/1065